# CHINESE
# New Year
## COLORING BOOK

**25 pages**

This book
belongs to:

○○○○○○○○○○○○○○○○○○○○○○

# TEST COLOR

# HORSE

# DRAGON

# MONKEY

# TIGER

RABBIT

RAT

# PIG

# ROOSTER

# SNAKE

# DRAGON

# HAPPY CHINESE NEW YEAR!

Please leave a
review -
I'd love to know it!

Made in the USA
Las Vegas, NV
11 January 2024

84174912R00031